LANDSLIDE

Contents

1 **The Discovery**   9
2 **Landslide**   17
3 **Searching for Survivors**   25
4 **A New Painting**   32
   Portalopedia   40

by Keira Wong
illustrated by Douglas Fong

SCHOLASTIC

Reading Manga: What is it?

The Japanese word 'manga' has been used for nearly 200 years. It means whimsical pictures (man = whimsical, ga = pictures).

Today, manga is a label for Japanese-style graphic novels, comic books and animated movies (also called anime). What's the difference between a graphic novel and a comic book? The answer is in your hands. Graphic novels are usually quality productions, sometimes run to hundreds of pages, and often cover serious subjects. Many Japanese manga focus on topics like the environment, the law, science, history – you name it.

Manga don't all look exactly the same, but they have some things in common:

Big Eyes

Oversized Expressions

Fast Action

Reading Manga: How to Follow

Each page of a graphic novel is divided into boxes called panels. You follow the panels from left to right and top to bottom, like this:

Each panel is like a paragraph in a regular book. It shows you where the characters are, and what they are doing, saying and thinking.

Some panels include a little box at the top (or the bottom), giving you information about what's going on. These are called captions.

DID YOU KNOW?

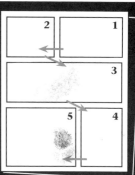

Traditional Japanese manga look a little different. That's because in Japan, people read from right to left. Japanese manga is read like this:

It's easier than it looks!

Reading Manga: Who's talking?

Speech balloons tell you who is speaking, what they're saying, and how.

Sometimes the lettering changes, to tell you which words are most important. These words might appear in **BOLD** or LARGE TYPE or in *ITALICS*.

Sometimes a punctuation point is enough to explain what's going on.

And how would you show an alien language? Maybe like this:

Reading Manga: What's that sound?

When you read speech bubbles, you hear manga characters' voices inside your head. There's a way to hear the background noises too – the rumble of thunder, the ringing of a telephone, the crack of a stick underfoot.

Manga artists represent sound effects (or SFX) by placing words over the panels, using lettering to suit each particular sound. It looks like this:

Scary sound

Mechanical sound

Quiet sound

DID YOU KNOW?

Japanese manga SFX are very precise. For example, *bicha bicha* means small splash, *bashan* is a medium splash, and *zaban* is a very big splash. There's even an SFX for total silence: *shiin*.

SFX are used to show emotions as well. The word *unzori* placed next to a character tells you they're feeling bored. If it was *moji moji* they'd be feeling shy, and *shobo shobo* indicates sadness.

Reading Manga:
What's that look on your face?

Manga characters have exaggerated expressions, to help you understand what they're feeling. The first feature everyone notices is the eyes, which may be wide open in:

Shock　　　　　　　Fear　　　　　　　Hope

Closed eyes can mean:

Laughter　　　　　　Sadness

Noses and chins are more difficult to spot (some characters have no nose at all). This reflects the Japanese preference for delicate features. In manga, big noses and chins are kept for the bad guys.

Reading Manga:

What's that look on your face?

Just like manga characters' eyes, manga mouths are either huge or tiny. A big, wide-open mouth indicates:

Fear Anger Happiness

A character with a little mouth may be feeling:

Sad Thoughtful Shy

You can also tell a lot about manga characters from the crazy colour or style of their hair. For example, blue hair can mean the character is cool-headed, while orange hair equals determination (and sometimes a fiery temper). Wild, spiky hairstyles show the character is adventurous.

Characters

Earthlings

Molly

Molly is sporty and adventurous and friendly to everyone – even aliens from strange planets.

James

Molly's friend James is always ready for a new challenge. Just as well.

Halycrusians

Z-koo

A Halycrusian leader, who is honest, fair-minded and keen to explore his world with Molly and James.

K-la

Z-koo's niece. She doesn't always think before acting, and this can lead to trouble …

B-roc

B-roc is a laid-back guy – always on the lookout for something to eat.

M-jie

The leader of the nomadic Halycrusians, who travel all corners of the planet.

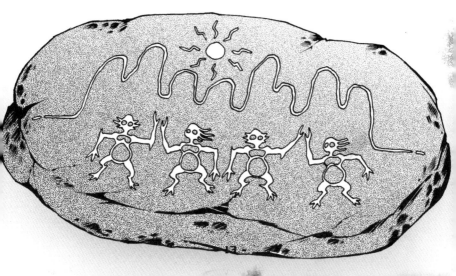

chapter 2 : Landslide

THE ROCK PAINTING IS CRUSHED.

chapter 4: A New Painting